Hard Loving

Hard
Loving

Poems by

MARGE PIERCY

WESLEYAN UNIVERSITY PRESS

Middletown, Connecticut

Grateful acknowledgement is made to the following magazines, in which some of these poems have appeared: *CAW!*, *Transatlantic Review*, *Prairie Schooner*, *31 New American Poets*, *The Carleton Miscellany*, *New: American and Canadian Poetry*, *Poltergeist*, *Apple*, *Premiere*, *Liberation News Service*, *The Minnesota Review*, *Epoch*, and *Leviathan*.

Special thanks are due to *Hanging Loose*, in which perhaps a fifth of these poems appeared.

Library of Congress Catalog Card Number: 70–82544

Manufactured in the United States of America

First edition

from the Movement
for the Movement

Contents

Hard Loving

1.

I could not tell
if I climbed up or down.
I could feel
that the ground
was not level
and often I stumbled.
I only knew
that the light was poor,
my hands damp
and sharp fears
sang, sang like crickets
in my throat.

2.

As I climb above the treeline
my feet are growing numb,
blood knocks in my wrists and forehead.
Voices chitter out of gnarled bushes.
I seem to be carrying
a great many useless objects,
a saw, a globe, a dictionary,
a doll leaking stuffing,
a bouquet of knitting needles,
a basin of dried heads.
Voices sigh from calendar pages
I have lived too long to love you.
Withered and hard as a spider
I crawl among bones:
awful charnel knowledge
of failure, of death, of decay.
I am old as stone.
Who can make soup of me?
A spider-peddler with pack of self

I scrabble under a sky of shame.
Already my fingers are thin as ice.
I must scuttle under a rock
and hide in webs
of mocking voices.

3.   *Meditation in my favorite position*

Peace, we have arrived.
The touch point
where words end
and body goes on.
That's all:
finite, all five-sensual
and never repeatable.
Know you and be known,
please you and be pleased
in act:
the antidote to shame
is nakedness together.
Words end,
body goes on
and something
small and wet and real
is exchanged.

4.

The eyes of others
measure and condemn.
The eyes of others are watches ticking no.
My friend hates you.
Between you I turn and turn
holding my arm as if it were broken.
The air is iron shavings polarized.
Faces blink on and off.

Words are heavy, heavy.
I carry them back and forth in my skirt.
They pile up in front of the chairs.
Words are bricks that seal the doors and windows.
Words are shutters on the eyes
and lead gloves on the hands.
The air is a solid block.
We cannot move.

5.

Sometimes your face
burns my eyes.
Sometimes your orange chest
scalds me.
I am loud and certain with strangers.
Your hands on the table
make me shy.
Your voice in the hall:
words rattle in my throat.
There is a bird in my chest
with wings too broad
with beak that rips me
wanting to get out.
I have called it
an idiot parrot.
I have called it
a ravening eagle.
But it sings.
Bird of no name
your cries are red and wet
on the iron air.
I open my mouth
to let you out
and your shining
blinds me.

6.
Suddenly I see it:
the gradual ease.
I no longer know how many times.
Afternoons blur into afternoons,
evenings melt into evenings.
Almost everyone guesses—
those who don't never will.
The alarms have stopped
except in my skin.
Tigers in a closet
we learn gentleness.
Our small habits together
are strange
as crows' tears
and easy as sofas.
Sometimes, sometimes
I can ask for what I want:
I have begun to trust you.

The death of the small commune

Loving feels lonely in a violent world,
irrelevant to people burning like last year's weeds
with bellies distended, with fish throats agape
and flesh melting down to glue.
We can no longer shut out the screaming
that leaks through the ventilation system,
the small bits of bone in the processed bread,
so we are trying to make a community
warm, loose as hair but shaped like a weapon.
Caring, we must use each other to death.
Love is arthritic. Mistrust swells like a prune.
Perhaps we gather so they may dig one big cheap grave.
From the roof of the Pentagon which is our Bastille
the generals armed like Martians watch through binoculars
the campfires of draftcards and barricades on the grass.
All summer helicopters whine over the ghetto.
Casting up jetsam of charred fingers and torn constitutions
the only world breaks on the door of morning.
We have to build our city, our camp
from used razorblades and bumpers and aspirin boxes
in the shadow of the nuclear plant that kills the fish
with coke bottle lamps flickering
on the chemical night.

Green the color of katydid

I was a rabbit with twigs for bones.
Drooling, pointing
dogs snuffled my tracks.
The sky struck white.
I learned to run.
Trap by the stream,
hawk in the sky,
I crouched in grasses smelling fear
till my belly
turned scum green,
but fever's sweat
oiled my ears
to catch the creak
of a grasshopper's jaw
and my eyes now
are sharp
as new pencils.

1. *Wee*

I am thin as nail parings. Light as dandruff.
When I cry I listen to myself,
pages of Bible paper turning over.

Who will love my morning toadstool sighs?
My rubber lusts sway like sea anenomes.
My hatreds mew once and stifle, still blind.

I will zip my mouth and put mittens on my hands
and innocent and eggstill I will wait.
On a teatray my vanilla prince will come.

2. *Whey*

Why do you cry? No one comes.
I am waiting in the grey to be born.

Your legs are driftwood.
Your face is a pike's.
Your touch rusts.
Why do you rub the mirror?
How could my hair thin when no one pulled it?
Whose fingers pressed in my cheeks?
What mousemouth sucked my breasts?
My shadow limps from the window baaing.
Fog is in me.

Who are you crying for? Ash
in the chimney flue.
The sun to fatten my shrunk shadow.
Quick, bear me: my gourd chest shakes.
The clock trickles sand on my forehead.
I am dry as onions.

See the sun's fatherly eye
opening to heat me.
Today is my right birthday.

Bury her.

Nobody understood Juan.
Slight, amiable, he did not stand upon ceremony
but was unfailingly polite.
Men liked him: he deferred with wry grace
though his pride was sore and supple with constant use.
He was fascinated by mirrors and women's eyes.
When he spoke of the past he was always alone
half in shadow among shadowy forms.
No one in his stories had names. No one had faces.
He watched himself but did not listen to his voice.
Words were water or weapons.
He was always in love with the body that burned his eyes.
His need shone in the dark and the light, always new.
He could not bear suspense or indifference.
He had to be closed into love on the instant
while his need gleamed like a knife and the words spurted.
He never understood what the women minded.
He never could see how he cheated them
with words, the mercury words no one could grasp
as they gleamed and slipped and darted.
In the woman's eyes he saw himself.
He was compiling a woman he would have to love.
He was building a woman out of a hill of bodies.
The sadness of his closets: hundreds of arms,
thousands of hollow and deflated breasts,
necks and thighs smooth as new cars,
forests of hair waving and limp.
Why do they mind? They do not learn.
Time after time they grapple to win back from him
what gleamed in his face before:
the mask of desperate beautiful need
which each woman claims.

They chase themselves through his hard flesh.
The bed is his mirror.
He spends into peace and indifference. He sleeps.
He is unfailingly polite, even with Donna Elvira
howling outside his door and breaking glass.
They always lose.

Man stomping over my bed in boots
carrying a large bronze church bell
which you occasionally drop:
gross man with iron heels
who drags coffins to and fro at four in the morning,
who hammers on scaffolding all night long,
who entertains sumo wrestlers and fat acrobats—
I pass you on the steps, we smile and nod.
Rage swells in me like gas.
Now rage too keeps me awake.

The friend

We sat across the table.
he said, cut off your hands.
they are always poking at things.
they might touch me.
I said yes.

Food grew cold on the table.
he said, burn your body.
it is not clean and smells like sex.
it rubs my mind sore.
I said yes.

I love you, I said.
that's very nice, he said
I like to be loved,
that makes me happy.
Have you cut off your hands yet?

Eleven-thirty and hot.
Cotton air.
Dry hands cupped.
The shadow of an empty chandelier
swings on a refrigerator door.
In the street a voice is screaming.
Your head scurries with ants.
Anyone's arms drip with your sweat,
anyone's pliant belly
absorbs your gymnastic thrusts
as your fury subsides into butter.
You are always in combat with questionnaires.
You are always boxing headless dolls
of cherry pudding.
You are the tedious marksman in a forest of thighs,
you with tomcat's shrapnel memory
and irritable eyes.
Tenderness is a mosquito on your arm.
Your hands are calloused with careless touch.
You believe in luck and a quick leap forward
that does not move you.
You rub your sore pride into moist bodies
and pedal off, slightly displeased.

Erasure

Falling out of love
is a rusty chain going quickly through a winch.
It hurts more than you will remember.
It costs a pint of blood turned grey
and burning out a few high paths
among the glittering synapses of the brain,
a few stars fading out at once in the galaxy,
a configuration gone
imagination called a lion or a dragon or a sunburst
that would photograph more like a blurry mouse.
When falling out of love is correcting vision
light grates on the eyes
light files the optic nerve hot and raw.
To find you have loved a coward and a fool
is to give up the lion, the dragon, the sunburst
and take away your hands covered with small festering bites
and let the mouse go in a grey blur
into the baseboard.

When I hug you, you are light as a grasshopper.
Your bones are ashwood the Indians used for bows,
you bend and spring back and can burn the touch,
a woman with hands that know how to pick things up.
Stiff as frozen rope words poke out
lopsided, in a fierce clothespin treble.
You move with a grace that is all function,
you move like a bow drawn taut and released.
Sometimes your wrists are transparent.
Sometimes an old buffalo man
frozen on the prairie stares from your face.
Your hair and eyes are the color of creek
running in the afternoon opaque under slanted sun.
You are stubborn and hardy as a rubber mat.
You are light as a paper airplane and as elegant
and you can fly.

The secret of moving heavy objects is balance, you said
in a grey loft full of your sculpture,
figures piercing or hung on boundaries,
leaping their thresholds, impaled on broken mirrors,
passing and gone into new space.
Objects born from you are mended, makeshift.
Their magic rides over rust and splinters and nails,
over shards of glass and cellophane beginning to rip.
Fragments of your work litter the banks of minor highways,
shattered faces of your icons lie on Hoboken junkyards,
float as smog over the East River,
grow black with the dust of abandoned coalbins.

One summer you made small rooms of wax
where people stood in taut ellipses staring and blind
with tenderness, with agony, with question and domestic terror.
They were candles burning.
You wanted to cast them in bronze but could not afford to.
The August sun melted them all.

The dancers in your plays move too in the dark
with masks and machines and chairs that trot and wail,
flimsy ragtag things that turn holy and dance
till no one is audience
but all grope and stumble in your world.
When you enter it is clear there is someone come,
no longer a woman, not wiry warm quick flesh
but a makeshift holy artifact
moving on the blank face of the dark as on a river:
ark, artifact, dancer of your own long breaking dance
which makes itself through you fiercely, totally passing in light
leaving you thin and darkened as burnt glass.

Wedding pictures

Susan at nineteen
plump as a roasted chicken
steams buttery biscuits
in a white dress.
You were ripe, overripe,
succulent as a burst apricot:
your body had swelled
and eaten you
into its sweet juiciness:
you
were a small hard green seed
deep inside,
a pale seed in a watermelon
almost drowned
in flesh.

Now all at once it is colder

You talk too much.
Like a film run backward your day gallops by
and you rush on as if interruptions would tear you.
You are burning, burning
dry and sudden as a parched weed.
The flash blinds you.
You hear only the crackling of your flesh
and the amphetamine rhythms of your own voice.
Your arm feels hard as varnish to my hand.
Come back, I say, I don't like where you're going.
You answer, come with me, hurry, we're leaving now!
A cinder blows in my eye.
A smell of singed wool makes me sneeze.
The last thing to fade
is the copter's whir of your voice still calling.
Did I listen hard enough?
What were you trying to say?
I think it was, Goodbye.
I think it sounded like, Help me.
It could have been, Give me your hand.
All I could hear in the crackling was, Hurry! Hurry!
and I saw no reason to hurry, then.

Trajectory of the traveling Susan

Round Susan, somewhere Susan,
Susan with suitcase and Berlitz book and stuffed shoulderbag
flies in the air sitting down.
Your spices are waiting under the falling dust,
your crippled roach peers waving feelers from behind a pot
while his hostile brothers prance on the burners.
Strange pussies are sticking their paws under the door.
Goss sits in a corner with his head loose in his hands
and plays at poking out his eyes.
The ceilings are blackboards he has scrawled with hieroglyphics.
The mailman fills up the box with nothing.

Quail Susan, pheasant Susan
riding an aluminum paperclip
between the cold stars and the jellyfish,
remember us in the broken net,
come back to us in the wooly strands of the caring web
stuck between jammed weeks and waiting testily.
Each love is singular.
The strands hang loose.

Apricot Susan, applesauce Susan
stuck up in the sky like a painted angel,
you think the web is a trap.
You see mouths open to swallow you in pieces.
You see gaping beaks and hear piercing cries of fill-me.
Susan, you are a hungry bird too with mouth wide open.
The nets we build never hold each other,
the minnow instant darts through the fingers
leaving a phosphorescent smear
and nothing else.
We must love each other and die.

Jagged Susan, enamel Susan,
Susan of sullen sleeps and jabbing elbows,
of lists and frenetic starts,
of the hiss of compressed air and the doors slide shut,
you can't hang in the air like a rainbow.
We are making the revolution out of each other.
We have no place else to begin
but with our hungers and our caring and our teeth.
Each love is singular
and the community still less than the addition of its parts.
We are each other's blocks and bricks.
To build a house we must first dig a hole
and try not to fall in.

The city lies grey and sopping like a dead rat
under the slow oily rain.
Between the lower east side tenements
the sky is a snotty handkerchief.
The garbage of poor living slimes the streets.
You lie on your bed and think
soon it will be hot and violent,
then it will be cold and mean.
You say you feel as empty
as a popbottle in the street.
You say you feel full of cold water
standing like an old horse trough.
The clock ticks, somewhat wrong,
the walls crack their dry knuckles.
Work is only other rooms where people cough,
only the typewriter clucking like a wrong clock.
Nobody will turn the soiled water into wine,
nobody will shout cold Lazarus alive
but you. You are your own magician.
Stretch out your hand,
stretch out your hand and look:
each finger is a snake of energy,
a gaggle of craning necks.
Each electric finger conducts the world.
Each finger is a bud's eye opening.
Each finger is a vulnerable weapon.
The sun is floating in your belly like a fish.
Light creaks in your bones.
You are sleeping with your tail in your mouth.
Unclench your hands and look.
Nothing is given us but each other.
We have nothing to give
but ourselves.
We have nothing to take but the time
that drips, drips anyhow

leaving a brown stain.
Open your eyes and your belly.
Let the sun rise into your chest and burn your throat,
stretch out your hands and tear the gauzy rain
that your world can be born from you
screaming and red.

When we are going toward someone we say
you are just like me
your thoughts are my brothers
word matches word
how easy to be together.

When we are leaving someone we say
how strange you are
we cannot communicate
we can never agree
how hard, hard and weary to be together.

We are not different nor alike
but each strange in his leather body
sealed in skin and reaching out clumsy hands
and loving is an act
that cannot outlive
the open hand
the open eye
the door in the chest standing open.

I am a light you could read by

A flame from each finger,
my hands are candelabra,
my hair stands in a torch.
Out of my mouth a long flame hovers.
Can't anyone see, handing me a newspaper?
Can't anyone see, stamping my book overdue?
I walk blazing along Sixth Avenue,
burning gas blue I buy subway tokens,
a bouquet of coals, I cross the bridge.
Invisible I singe strangers and pass.
Now I am on your street.
How your window flickers.
I come bringing my burning body
like an armful of tigerlilies,
like a votive lantern,
like a roomful of tassels and leopards and grapes
for you to come into,
dance in my burning
and we will flare up together like stars
and fall to sleep.

One night in January
in the middle of sore times
I lay in your arms
too taut with joy
to douse in sleep
in the morning brown eggs
you sang in the kitchen come
if you want to, come
and the night and the morning
a tough tall raggedy flower
a flag red hollyhock
sprung from snow and asphalt
you leapt in my arms
I danced in your skin
the sun stood still
at the pole of night
we knocked like balloons
against the ceiling
all the night and the morning
burning but softly
without smoke or ash
bursting in rough bloom
out of ice and asphalt
pomegranate red
one January night.

The fisherman

You are trawling with a fine net in your depths.
Up they come and spill on the varnished deck
and their phosphorescence dims
and their colors begin to fade,
shy creatures who swell and burst,
tenuous flimsy beasts that shrivel and dry up
till all die gasping.
See! you address the stinking pile,
you are not real.

There and not there,
you kept fading into your smoky flesh
to charge out butting.
You acted as if my face were a barb
you might catch on,
as if out of bed
if you recognized me
I might charge you something.
I ran into you too fast
without stopping to look
at the signs, the weather,
the way the clouds loomed and toppled.
I find myself in a revolving door
in the middle of a field
close to the daisies, the long rolling grasses
trapped between blades of glass turning.

Easy

How easy it is to be happy
you say sometimes,
chocolate afternoons,
the summer sun of our bodies,
rarely a whole night
big as the biggest pumpkin.
We can eat it all.
Playing in the streets
I am shy
because you are so beautiful
women want to attack me
with envy
with purses and nails.
I should whisper to them
no, no, he is not mine
we are guests together
but still, how easy
easy as butter
easy as silk and honey
to turn and touch you
you, sometimes
when you really look back at me
when you really see me
and be happy
at once, like eating icecream.

Your eyes are hard, and other surprises

Will the white sun rise?
Throat packed with salt and rockdust.
My cactus eyes.

Someone has twisted my shadow.
Small and smaller, hunchbacked it drags.
Where will it go?

In closets I plead my case,
in toilet stalls, in furnace rooms.
My smiling face

unpeels in hanging strips.
Words that foam and dry and harden
tear my lips.

Hey my enemy, whose hate
sleets on me, do the hairs of your belly
remember my sweat?

I still feel you

Like a fishbone in my throat
or one of your hairs that used to catch in my teeth
a piece of iron is traveling through my muscles,
a bit of jagged iron,
an end of harpoon or a broken hook.
Now it sticks as I catch my breath.
Now as I run downstairs it bites my instep.
Now it is tunneling through my belly.
It leaks a slow rust into the blood,
a sad dark orange taste on my tongue
acid but meek.
Blindly this metal remnant wanders in me
as you did, blindly taking the easiest way
in or out
whether you found an opening,
orifice or old wound,
or had to cut one.

The death of the small commune

The death of the small commune
is almost accomplished.
I find it hard now to believe
in connection beyond the couple,
hard as broken bone.
Time for withdrawal and healing.
Time for lonely work
spun out of the torn gut.
Time for touching turned up earth,
for trickling seed from the palm,
thinning the shoots of green herb.
What we wanted to build
was a way station for journeying
to a new world,
but we could not agree long enough
to build the second wall,
could not love long enough
to move the heavy stone on stone,
not listen with patience
to make a good plan,
we could not agree.
Nothing remains but a shallow hole,
nothing remains
but a hole
in everything.

Loving an honest man

Two A.M. laundry bleach moonlight
pits the crabbed
and hunchbacked houses.
A snuffling yard engine,
mother cat drunk with sneezing,
shuttles cars.
Our steps creak.
We breathe ghosts.
By the jagged shadow of a hedge,
look, a rabbit crouches.
Ears of lilies.
His nose steams.
As I watch him, ice
gnaws the rim of my eyes.
The air smells like coal.
How does he live?
What hunts him?
Will you touch me?

Missing person

When you are off in another city
that city is lit up like a gold tooth,
a whistle blowing orange in the corner of my mind.
The earth is lopsided toward Boston.
People in the street swarm up invisible hills.
I am walking crooked:
my head leans north.
Nothing is uglier than a beige telephone
hiding you inside
squat and smug and miserly
with the dial of a combination lock on a safe.
Sleepwalking I dream of a city that clucks like a hen
covering you with feathery smoke and barnred houses.
Stalled between day and night,
numbed by exhaust fumes, dulled by waiting,
time without you I walk through a tunnel
where anxieties drip and stain the walls
and fans beat the air like drowning swimmers.
A tunnel is between, a tunnel ends,
I cannot get lost in a tunnel
but not until the last turn
can I see light.

In the bedroom dense with feathers and smell of sex
we turn. One of us starts it,
an accusation in letters of black flame.
A monumental bill covers the ceiling,
shock scorches the air,
everything hums and has edges of blue light.
We both hope it will stop and leap at each other.
Sharks, we thrash in the darkening sea,
your teeth are in my throat,
I am ripping your flank.
Down we plunge churning and tearing
while the banner of our blood
flares on the whirlpool.
The pain is an avalanche,
the pain roars and blackens everything.
Entrails float around us.
We must both be dead.
Then we are paddling with broad porpoise grins
breaking the surface to leap,
sleek and totally erogenous and rough.
A dangerous way to get clean:
the smell of blood attracts hungry fish.
But how else to cut through the barnacles and the slime,
the scabs and toughening hide of each day?
How, unless we are willing to fight to the bone,
can we ever find each other naked?

Bronchitis on the 14th floor

The air is full of piranhas
disguised as snow.
In the red chair my cat
licks her buttery paw.
My fever has ripened like a pear.
A bubble of oxygen,
I percolate in clogged lungs,
I simmer in sweet fat
above the flickering city.
The shocked limb of Broadway
flutters spasmodically below.
My lungs shine, two lanterns.
I love the man who stands
at the foot of my bed
whose voice tumbles like a bear
over the ceiling,
whose hands smell of tangerines and medicine.
Through nights of fire and grit
streaked with falling claws
he carries me golden with fever
safely, swiftly forward
on the galloping sleigh of our bed.

How we marry each other

All the time you are gone
I am braiding a charm in the hair of my belly
smelling of fear and myself.
While you are cut from my side sleep won't cover me.
My breath all night is folded and starched,
bad dreams hatch termites in my spine.
We never write each other letters:
we produce no souvenirs.

You walk flatfooted.
Your hair blows in wisps.
Your voice makes plaster fall.
Your belly seamed by a scar puckers the tongue.
The dunes of your shoulders are honey and coarse grass.
You taste of lemon and leather and salt.
After we have made love
your sex crouches on you still swollen
a red pelican subjugating you too.
You are paced in your joy,
you control and watch and ride in my lurching tides
then open, groaning in a rush of semen hot as blood
given, given, like a man falling.

Now with an umbrella half open in my throat
I expect the cough of your key.
Waiting is a pain that goes out all at once
like a bad noise.
Now I can breathe, now we are enlaced and functioning.
In a short while we will be able
to walk about freely in our clothes in front of others
pretending tolerance, pretending to be married
concealing that transparent elastic fold
of Siamese skin.

Crabs

They are light as flakes of dandruff with scrawny legs.
Like limpets they cling to the base of each curly hair,
go lurching among the underbrush for cover.
Our passions are their weathers.
Coitus is the Santa Maria hitting on virgin land,
an immigrant ship coming into harbor,
free homesteads for all.
Or native crabs vs. conquistadors wrestle and nip.
Or maybe they too mingle.
As the boat glides in, there they are, the native crabs
with mandolins and bouquets of bougainvillaea
swaying on the dock singing Aloha.
For three generations we haven't seen a new face.
O the boredom, the stale genes, the incest.
Or perhaps when the two shores approach
the crabs line up to leap the gap like monkeys,
the hair always lusher on the other side.
They travel as fast as gossip.
They multiply like troubles.
They cling and persist through poison and poking and picking,
dirt and soap, torrents and drought,
like love or any other stubborn itch.

There are eight people in this room.
I am loving five of them
whether they like it or not and often they don't,
being hopped by an electric windmill with cowbells,
a rain of salamanders and feather beds and overripe onions.
My loving is a sweaty tango with a python
among the marshmallow bushes, I know it.
Today two of these people filmed a girl with a smile
trying to give dollars or flowers to passersby
who ducked their heads and hustled on.
There is no love without its coercion,
there are no gifts without taxes.
Nothing belongs to me except my hands
and I go around trying to give them away.
A spare hand in the house, nasty, curious as a monkey,
you couldn't keep it in a cage. What would it eat?
It would probably break things.
It is probably better to lock the door.

Loving an honest man

So we live with each other: not against
not over or under or in tangent.
Secretive in joy and touching, back to back
sensual taproot feeding deep in the soil
we face out with hands open and usually bruised,
crafting messages of lightning in common brick.

Working, you shout, pace, pound the blackboard.
Chalk goes to pieces in your hand
like a giggling girl.
But the cost-effective men close in.
The ordnance makers hitch your ideas
as kite tails to missiles.
You sicken with the smog of machines charring the air
for no man's good
except the absent owners of everything.
A slow anger has drawn you lean,
sketched on your broad forehead the cost of trouble
in that mart where men are weighed and everything priced
including your head, in which coalescing systems
that shimmer like orange algae revolve, giving light.
An artist painted an abstract that a general bought.
In its honor the general had a small country
bombed into a reproduction.

Counting your wounds with my fingers, counting, counting.
How a man learns to stare at his hands
when he see his work taken and used
as machines for converting pain into money.
Vulnerable, open, a man with care slashed in your face,
you live with me touching and journeying
with the garish blood of defeat
splashed over our small sky like a horse opera sunset.

Unborn children who grow out of liberated earth
receive the artifacts of our lives in your curious hands
and turn over with respect these rough arrowheads.
Take and try this bow strung with human gut,
warm in your hands this ax made from a spine:
you grow out of us who love freedom and each other.

This is a poem for you

This is a poem for me
when the clock of my muscles runs down,
when my brain is a sponge oozing vinegar,
when I cover the mirror to lock in the ghosts.
This is a poem for you
after they have broken our heads and bodies,
when we are grey numbers in grey prisons,
when we are scattered in dusty cafes in dead-end freighter
     ports.
Remember that we were most beautiful not by twos,
never in formless plenaries or mumbly caterpillar meetings
but in small high holy groups shifting like starfish.
In odds and end rooms off insecticide corridors,
in dim lofts among lumber
we dance and touch in pulsing circles.
Our faces rise up soft and blurred with laughter.
Our faces float jagged with sudden wanting.
We shimmer with sweat.
We are playing out our knowledge of each other.
We are asking riddles with our hands
and solving them with our hips.
We are a soft clumsy organism.
Music blows through the long tangled pelt,
the red mouth is open to roar and taste,
the eyes are wide and bright and moist,
the paws are raised.

Somewhere in the tunnel of winter
the machines of hope turned off and the air went bad.
Too many lies had been handed you like canapés to eat.
Each defeat was small, each endurable one by one by one
till a mountain of dead roaches blocked your way.
You turned aside crying, Nothing matters except people.
You thought your love a gift friends would receive gladly
like a blank check,
but each asked only, What do you want for this?
Slowly you closed down to a charged coil of pain.
Then the spark leapt the gap at me, burning.
We fought and ripped till the blood broke through the skin
and the nerves went off like sirens
and the old and new wounds lit up in the dark like eyes.
Slowly we gathered each other's dismembered body,
knit the mangled limbs,
closing each wound with mouth and fingers and hair,
a slow underwater dance in the other's eyes.
Love, my love, my love, you have come back
but it is a planet with different colored sea and skies,
strange bright birds to sing, and new sweet and bitter fruit.
Healing, we are a new animal with new instincts and strengths
and nothing feels or tastes the same
except our love.

Curse of the earth magician

Address to the players

The Sphynx of the Pentagon squats on the Arlington shore.
What walks on men in the morning,
wades in corpses at noon,
flies over ashes at night?
Whose acid dissolves faces?
Whose box am I living in?
I cannot fight it till I name it.
My blood is programmed.
I must tear slowly each muscle
to pull the steel fibers from the flesh
grafted all the long years of growing upsidedown,
of growing against the crushing pressure
in the lightless seabottom cities of America.
Who owns my hands?
Can I steal them back?
We are playing in the streets
with banners and bells and billyclubs.
Blood squirts on the cement.
We are playing a dance in the streets
between the cops and the troops.
Who owns the teargas cannisters?
The arm of the boy holding the rifle shakes.
We must name the giant in whose belly we are chained.
We must put up the faces of hooded lords
on streetlamps and phonebooths and subway tiles.
You think you can go back to sleep.
You think you can dance for a while, then buy a house.
But your brain belongs to the king of the mines,
your body is his grass to mow in its ripeness,
your nerves are gadgets to pick and program.
There is only one choice. Call it freedom.
It is your head you are playing for.
Win or die.

Fathers and sons

Abraham laboring for dominion and increase
came to the rich moist land of grasses
after walking the desert of cackling sky
where the sun beat on stone gongs
dry as his throat, his palms, his eyes.
Abraham laboring to satisfaction and increase
worked the valleys and subjugated the hills,
sent the unclean into exile,
saw his worth grow with the seasons
and in winter begot a son.
His son increased
who had never drunk sheep piss for thirst,
who had never seen his hard-tried men and flocks
fall shrunken on the stones.
His son sat up all night with friends
discussing how he would redistribute the land,
make peace with small dark hill people
who used stone axes and died slowly.
When the challenge came
Abraham met it with his best.
He did not allow opportunity for debate
though while the knife was at the boy's throat
he made a short heartfelt speech
about dedication.

Learning experience

The boy sits in the classroom
in Gary, in the United States, in NATO, in SEATO
in the thing-gorged belly of the sociobeast
in fluorescent light in slowly moving time
in boredom thick and greasy as vegetable shortening.
The classroom has green boards and ivory blinds,
the desks are new and the teachers not so old.
I have come out on the train from Chicago to talk
about dangling participles. I am supposed
to teach him to think a little on demand.
The time of tomorrow's draft exam is written on the board.
The boy yawns and does not want to be in the classroom in
    Gary
where the furnaces that consumed his father seethe rusty smoke
and pour cascades of nerve-bright steel
while the slag goes out in little dumpcars smoking,
but even less does he want to be in Today's Action Army
in Vietnam, in the Dominican Republic, in Guatemala,
in death that hurts.
In him are lectures on small groups, Jacksonian democracy,
French irregular verbs, the names of friends
around him in the classroom in Gary in the pillshaped afternoon
where tomorrow he will try and fail his license to live.

The morning half-life blues

Girls buck the wind in the grooves toward work
in fuzzy coats promised to be warm as fur.
The shop windows snicker
flashing them hurrying over dresses they cannot afford:
you are not pretty enough, not pretty enough.

Blown with yesterday's papers through the boiled coffee morning
they dream of the stop on the subway without a name,
the door in the heart of the grove of skyscrapers,
that garden where we nestle to the teats of a furry world,
lie in mounds of peony eating grapes,
and need barter ourselves for nothing,
not by the hour, not by the pound, not by the skinful,
that party to which no one will give or sell them the key
though we have all thought briefly we had found it
drunk or in bed.

Black girls with thin legs and high necks stalking like herons,
plump girls with blue legs and green eyelids and strawberry
      breasts,
swept off to be frozen in fluorescent cubes,
the vacuum of your jobs sucks your brains dry
and fills you with the ooze of melted comics.
Living is later. This is your rented death.
You grasp at specific commodities and vague lusts
to make up, to pay for each day
which opens like a can and is empty, and then another,
afternoons like dinosaur eggs stuffed with glue.

Girls of the dirty morning, ticketed and spent,
you will be less at forty than at twenty.
Your living is a waste product of somebody's mill.
I would fix you like buds to a city where people work
to make and do things necessary and good,
where work is real as bread and babies and trees in parks
and you would blossom slowly and ripen to sound fruit.

The organizer's bogeymen

1. *Futility*

This meeting has gone on with small interruptions
for eleven years and part of another.
I classify the speakers in small bags.
The words come out in paragraphs shaped by use.
The words stain the room like dirty water.
We all have scars.
When we stand up we show them perfunctorily.
We finger them when others speak too long.
The ten of us remaining from ten thousand
have all betrayed each other.
We come from peddling our lost future on the streets
beside Jesus Saves and stolen watches.
Every one of us is chairman in his head.
The editor of the encyclopedia of expelled factions
has deciphered a new error:
he points his knotted finger.
Then we are up and screaming like gulls
wheeling over a liner's fresh garbage.
Then we are nine.
One takes notes and applauds:
he is the agent.
I no longer remember when I first heard myself say *we* and
     mean *no one*.

2. *Prison*

The cell as coffin,
time as decay,
the self as conscious worm:
I am afraid of prison.
Alone I am a spider
run out of spit to spin with,
clinging with eight crooked legs
to a cold blank of now.

It's true walls scare me,
the man's iron routine,
the lard of boredom,
head softening inside like an overripe melon,
fingers scrabbling at salty flesh,
but my reality, my sanity
is other people.
Blindness loud as hunger hollows me.
Light breaks from the faces that I love.
I cannot live
out of that sun.

3. *Exile*

You walk through streets that itch in your nose
where children's cries are strange moths.
If you bump hard into someone
his cry is different
from your cry.
You take monthold newspapers like benzedrine
waking dry excitations
numbed in stale argument.
Every banal tourist
is a messenger from a battle
where friends
who do not remember
are impaled.
You are always a child in another language,
you are someone else.
On the sidewalks a ghostly city
is printed on the learned routine of this:
in dreams you are always back there,
in dreams you speak American.
The politics of the exile are fever,
revenge, daydream,
theater of the aging convalescent.
You wait in the wings and rehearse.
You wait and wait.

Grey clouds sink.
All day from my hotel room
I watch the grey lake rise.
I rub and blow on inkstained fingers
patient as that wading stork.
Fog creeps in the window.
Smoke spools out.
From the cracked egg
of looted synagogue
weeds sprout in the rain.
In the glass and concrete orphanage
girls are learning to weave rugs
to sell to tourists.
It is not so bad, they say.
The soldier said the same,
hitchhiking toward his village
of rocks and gnarled shepherds,
about the army. The equipment
is new and American.
The army is a major industry
as under the Turks,
as under the Germans.
I am American and a tourist.
I am learning something about wet
and grey and bad.

Homo faber: the shell game

Pyramids of flesh sweat pyramids of stone.
Each slave chiseled his cheap as dust life in rock,
with labor dragged from him he marked his own grave
heaped over the painted chrysalis.
The Roman slaves built stadia and roads for empire and trade.
Cathedrals: parallel vaulted hands the color of winter clouds
where choirs of polyphonic light strike chilly slabs
while nobles with swords on and skinny saints lie under the
    floor.
Fortresses, dungeons, keeps, moats and walls.
Skyscrapers where nobody lives filled with paper.
Where do the people live and what have they made themselves
splendid as these towers of glass, these groves of stone?
The impulse that in 1910 molded banks as temples,
where now does it build its central artifact?
The ziggurat, the acropolis, the palace of our dream
whose shape rings in the blood's cave like belladonna,
all scream in the eagle's preyseeking swoop of the bomber,
those planes expensive as cities,
the sharklean submarines of death,
the taut kinetic tower of the missile,
the dark fiery omphalos of the bomb.

Morning rattles the tall spike fence.
Already the old are set out to get dirty in the sun
spread like drying coverlets around the garden
by straggly hedges smelling of tomcat.
From the steep oxblood hospital
hunched under its miser's frown of roof,
dishes mutter, pumps work, an odor
of disinfectant slops into the street
toward the greygreen quadrangles of the university.
Pickets with the facts of their poverty hoisted on sticks
turn in the street like a tattered washing.
The trustees decline to negotiate
for this is a charitable institution.

Among the houses of the poor and black nearby
a crane nods waisthigh among broken bedrooms.
Already the university digs foundations
to be hallowed with the names of old trustees.
The dish and bottle washers, the orderlies march
carrying the crooked sick toward death on their backs.
The neighborhood is being cured of poverty.
Busses will carry the moppushers in and out.

Are the old drying too slowly in their garden?
Under elms spacious and dusty
as roominghouse porches the old men mutter
that they are closing the north wing,
for the land is valuable when you get down to it
and they will, down to the prairie dog bones.

This is the Home for Incurables: and the old are.
Many are the diseases that trustees are blind to,
or call incurable, like their own blindness
wide as the hoarse wind blows, mile after mile
where the city smokes sweetly as a barbecue
or sizzles like acid under nobody's sun.

Why the soup tastes like the Daily News

The great dream stinks like a whale gone aground.
Somewhere in New York Harbor
in the lee of the iron maiden
it died of pollution
and was cast up on Cape Cod by the Provincetown Light.
The vast blubber is rotting.
Scales of fat ripple on the waters
until the taste of that decay
like a sulphurous factory of chemical plenty
dyes every tongue.

To grow on

The first chickyellow probes of sun
fluffy with mopdust
touch the windows.
Nothing here is quite
smooth or whole.
The pipes weep rust,
boards sag and heave,
plaster sighs into dust
and from the ceiling tatter
winsome stalactites
of paint.

On the ledges
old paint blisters into maps.
Chips of pretty paint
snow on the crib.
Paint, the landlord's friend,
holds up the walls.
All winter children peck it.

In the first cornsyrup pools of sun
small fingers uncoil
like germinating beans.
Fingers: test tubes
for that simple chemistry:
sun activates the lead
winter's swallowed drifts
whose tired colors now
run through the blood.

Death blooms with the
suburban hyacinths.
Even spring
charges a little more
to the poor.

Curse of the earth magician on a metal land

Marching, a dream of wind in our chests,
a dream of thunder in our legs,
we tied up midtown Manhattan for half an hour,
the Revolutionary Contingent and Harlem,
but it did not happen
because it was not reported in any newspaper.
The riot squad was waiting at the bottom of 42nd Street
to disperse us into uncertain memory.
A buffalo said to me
I used to crop and ruminate on LaSalle Street in Chicago
and the grasses were sweet under the black tower of the Board
    of Trade.
Now I stand in the zoo next to the yaks.
Let the ghosts of those recently starved rise
and like piranhas in ten seconds flat chew down to public bones
the generals and the experts on anti-personnel weapons
and the senators and the oil men and the lobbyists
and the sleek smiling sharks who dance at the Diamond Ball.
I am the earth magician about to disappear into the ground.
This is butterfly's war song about to disappear into the fire.
Put the eagle to sleep.
I see from the afternoon papers
that we have bought another country
and are cutting the natives down to build jet airstrips.
A common motif in monumental architecture in the United
    States
is an eagle with wings spread, beak open
and the globe grasped in his claws.
Put the eagle to sleep.
This is butterfly's war song addressed to the Congress of Sharks.
You are too fat, you eat bunches of small farmers like radishes
    for breakfast.
You are rotting our teeth with sugar
refined from the skulls of Caribbean children. Thus far

we have only the power of earth magicians, dream and song
and marching,
to dance the eagle to sleep.
We are about to disappear into the fire.
There is only time for a brief curse by a chorus of ghosts
of Indians murdered with smallpox and repeating rifles on the
plains,
of Indians shot by the marines in Santo Domingo,
napalmed in the mountains of Guatemala last week.
There will be no more spring.
Your corn will sprout in rows and the leaves will lengthen
but there will be no spring running clean water through the
bones,
no soft wind full of bees, no long prairie wind bearing feathers
of geese.
It will be cold or hot. It will step on your necks.
A pool of oil will hang over your cities,
oil slick will scum your lakes and streams killing the trout and
the ducklings,
concrete and plastic will seal the black earth and the red earth,
your rivers hum with radioactivity and the salmon float belly
up,
and your mountains be hollowed out to hold the files of great
corporations,
and shale oil sucked from under the Rockies till the continent
buckles.
Look! children of the shark and the eagle
you have no more spring. You do not mind.
You turn on the sunlamp and the airconditioning
and sit at the television watching the soldiers dance.

1.

HELP STOP WETNESS
cried the arid ad in the subway.
I used to go from you last year
and as the bus lurched west
from the looseness of my flesh
and the salty damp of my thighs
I would take comfort.
Wet is what flows and seeps and comes again:
the ocean we carry in us
where we spawned
to nourish life among alien rocks.
Even the trees cup sap that rises and falls.
Wet and sloppy the mutual joy
of stirring bodies together
warm as breast milk.
We are wet jokes and wet dreams.
A scalpel slits us open
like a busted bag of groceries
and out we ooze.
Noses drip. Armpits weep.
Man is born from a small salt pond.
Yet immersed in our own element we drown.
Men have no natural habitat.
Men have no home.
We have been making one badly for millennia.
The great contrary project
is to dry up the world
and turn everyone into machines for making money.

2.

The wise ones a million years past
went home again.
Dolphins have no houses, no coins,

no tools, no storage bins.
Civilization is the attempt
to survive hideless in the barren air.
Dolphins in the sea help one another.
Man among rocks and cement
fears man worse than the cyclone.
The traditional way of making do up here
is to turn your neighbors into cattle,
hire guards with clubs to herd them
and milk them
and slaughter them.
We incorporate ten thousand years of bad habits.
Habits of men pretending to be cattle.
Habits of men who use others to fatten on.

3.

We have only just arrived, a few scouts
from the mountains of scarcity
to the plains of abundance.
It is time to turn over.
It is time to loosen and to make new.
We are sacs of mad cells that have forgotten how to grow.
It is time to close ourselves to the steel probes
of the corporate generals and devisers.
It is time to open ourselves to the other with respect.
Time for the sea of mankind to rise and roll.
Time to learn how we are part of one wave and each other.
Sisters and brothers in movement,
we carry in the wet cuneiform of proteins
the long history of working to be human.
In this time we shall fail into ashes,
fail into metal and dry bones and paper,
or break through into a sea of shared abundance
where man shall join man

in salty joy, in flowing trust.
We must be healed at last to our soft bodies
and our hard planet
to make live and conscious history in common.

Distinguished contemporary poetry in cloth and paperback editions

ALAN ANSEN: *Disorderly Houses* (1961)

JOHN ASHBERY: *The Tennis Court Oath* (1962)

ROBERT BAGG: *Madonna of the Cello* (1961)

MICHAEL BENEDIKT: *The Body* (1968)

ROBERT BLY: *Silence in the Snowy Fields* (1962).

GRAY BURR: *A Choice of Attitudes* (1969)

TURNER CASSITY: *Watchboy, What of the Night?* (1966)

TRAM COMBS: *saint thomas. poems.* (1965)

DONALD DAVIE: *Events and Wisdoms* (1965); *New and Selected Poems* (1961)

JAMES DICKEY: *Buckdancer's Choice* (1965) [National Book Award in Poetry, 1966]; *Drowning With Others* (1962); *Helmets* (1964)

DAVID FERRY: *On the Way to the Island* (1960)

ROBERT FRANCIS: *The Orb Weaver* (1960)

JOHN HAINES: *Winter News* (1966).

EDWIN HONIG: *Spring Journal: Poems* (1968)

RICHARD HOWARD: *The Damages* (1967); *Quantities* (1962)

BARBARA HOWES: *Light and Dark* (1959)

DAVID IGNATOW: *Figures of the Human* (1964); *Rescue the Dead* (1968); *Say Pardon* (1961)

DONALD JUSTICE: *Night Light* (1967); *The Summer Anniversaries* (1960) [A Lamont Poetry Selection]

CHESTER KALLMAN: *Absent and Present* (1963)

PHILIP LEVINE: *Not This Pig* (1968)

LOU LIPSITZ: *Cold Water* (1967)

JOSEPHINE MILES: *Kinds of Affection* (1967)

VASSAR MILLER: *My Bones Being Wiser* (1963); *Onions and Roses* (1968); *Wage War on Silence* (1960)

W. R. MOSES: *Identities* (1965)

LEONARD NATHAN: *The Day the Perfect Speakers Left* (1969)

DONALD PETERSEN: *The Spectral Boy* (1964)

MARGE PIERCY: *Breaking Camp* (1968); *Hard Loving* (1969)

HYAM PLUTZIK: *Apples from Shinar* (1959)

VERN RUTSALA: *The Window* (1964)

HARVEY SHAPIRO: *Battle Report* (1966)

JON SILKIN: *Poems New and Selected* (1966)

LOUIS SIMPSON: *At the End of the Open Road* (1963) [Pulitzer Prize in Poetry, 1964]; *A Dream of Governors* (1959)

ANNE STEVENSON: *Reversals* (1969)

RICHARD TILLINGHAST: *Sleep Watch* (1969)

JAMES WRIGHT: *The Branch Will Not Break* (1963); *Saint Judas* (1959); *Shall We Gather at the River* (1968)